Original title:
100% Sure I Have No Idea What's Going On

Copyright © 2025 Creative Arts Management OÜ
All rights reserved.

Author: Seraphina Caldwell
ISBN HARDBACK: 978-1-80566-109-2
ISBN PAPERBACK: 978-1-80566-404-8

## A Path Paved with Questions

Why does my sock always go astray?
Is it running to join a parade today?
The toaster mocks me with its brownish fame,
While I'm just here, still searching for the game.

A cat in a hat, oh what a sight!
Stealing my snacks, with unusual delight.
Every time I think I've got it on track,
Life flips the script, it's all just a snack.

## **Fleeting Glimpses of Truth**

I catch a glimpse of knowledge, small and bright,
But it slips away in the dim morning light.
Like bubbles that pop, ideas come and flee,
Leaving me wondering what's next, can't you see?

The clock ticks loudly, a jester in disguise,
Each tick a riddle, oh how time flies!
I try to catch answers, with a butterfly net,
But they laugh and tease, well, not a single bet.

## The Landscape of the Bewildered

I walk through fields of upside-down thoughts,
Where daisies wear bows and tie knots.
The sunflowers giggle, they must know the score,
While I'm just lost at the puzzling door.

Clouds skip by, wearing silly hats,
I ask them directions, they just laugh like brats.
A squirrel holds court, tells tales of the wise,
But his nuggets of wisdom, oh what a surprise!

## The Puzzle of Presence

Here I am, stuck in an endless charade,
Trying to decipher the mess I've made.
I can't find the corners, nor edges, nor folds,
It's a jigsaw of moments that never unfolds.

A duck in a tie quacks wisdom so proud,
"Get your act together!" it says, oh so loud.
But wading through nonsense is what I prefer,
In this quirky delight, I just want to stir.

## Whirlwinds of Reflection

In a world that spins like a top,
I chase my tail, then take a hop.
Thoughts collide, like cats at play,
Twisted paths lead me astray.

Questions float like butterflies,
Answering them feels like a prize.
Looking up, then looking down,
Jester's cap, my crown of frown.

Maps unfold with no direction,
Lost in thought, what a complexion!
Giggles burst, a sneaky sigh,
What is truth? Just a pie in the sky.

In the mirror, faces tease,
Whisper secrets, aims to please.
Lost in laughter, I cringe and dance,
Round and round, in a silly trance.

## **Dancing with Ambivalence**

Two left feet and a sprightly heart,
Do I start here, or part with my part?
Twists and turns in the dizzy air,
Step to the left, but who's really there?

A jigsaw puzzle of mismatched clues,
Do I wear the red, or dance in my blues?
With every dip, my mind goes blank,
Twirl again, ship's anchor sank.

Frolicking doubts parade in line,
Is this the path, or just a sign?
Catch my breath, then lose the beat,
Laughing loud, feel the heat.

Mixed signals paint a vibrant scene,
In shadows cast, I chase the keen.
Together we trip on the edge of the mundane,
Tap-tap-tap, like a runaway train.

# **Fractured Certainties**

Stand on a tower of thought like a fool,
Trying to swim in a bath of drool.
A map of stars all turned to dust,
Waving my hands, it's a must.

One shoe's on, the other's a ghost,
In the game of life, I play the host.
Round and round, the questions loop,
In chaos's grip, I take a soup.

Colors clash like zebras in grey,
I answer questions in a quirky way.
What was the question? I lost my thread,
Oh look, there's a fish wearing bread.

In a maze of bits and pieces,
Confusion grows as clarity ceases.
Join the dance with a wobbly cheer,
Trust the process, if you dare near.

## Voices in the Silence

Whispers echo in my busy head,
Tickle my thoughts, where have they led?
Silly voices make me laugh,
In quietude, they draft a path.

What's that sound? Is it a clue?
Or just the echoes of my shoe?
Holding court with ghosts of doubt,
Joking round, they laugh and shout.

Silent chaos spins around,
In muted tones, I've finally found.
A symphony of thoughts awry,
Singing sweet where worries lie.

Mirth and mayhem in a playful tone,
In the stillness, I find my own.
Listen closely, the world anew,
There's laughter here, and joy through and through.

## Where Clarity Dares Not Tread

In a world where logic takes a break,
Each thought's a ripple in the lake.
With cues so lost, like socks in dryers,
I search for sense, like solving choirs.

The calendar ticks, but I sit still,
Wondering what's next, and if it will.
My brain's a circus, all clowns and jest,
Trying to find what I know best.

Questions float like balloons in air,
I grasp at one; it leads to despair.
Is this a riddle or just a joke?
I laugh so hard, it nearly chokes.

Yet amidst the chaos, a giggle grows,
In the land of mystery, anything goes.
With every twist, my mind spins round,
I raise a toast to the lost and found.

## **Mysterious Maps of Mind**


I hold a map with clouds and stars,
Leading to places, near and far.
But every path seems to take a turn,
Is that a landmark or just a fern?

Each crumpled edge tells tales untold,
Of ships that sailed and knights so bold.
But in this maze of thought and whim,
I can't help but feel a little dim.

A compass spins, but it won't decide,
If left is right, or if I should hide.
The GPS blinks and mocks my plight,
I'm more lost now than day or night.

Yet laughter bubbles in the deepest strife,
As I wander through this strange life.
With every misstep, I find more cheer,
In the jumbled maps of thoughts unclear.

## Riddles Wrapped in Shadows

In the corner lurks a riddle dark,
Its whispers tickle like a lark.
I turn to face this shadow's jest,
Its laughter lingers, never rests.

Questions wrapped in mystery's cloak,
Like clouds that tease the sun's warm poke.
I squint and guess, but can't unwind,
What's hidden deep within my mind.

A puzzle box without the key,
Its secrets giggle back at me.
With every clue, confusion grows,
A game where no one really knows.

Yet here I stand, a merry fool,
Embracing chaos as my rule.
In shadows deep, I'll dance and sway,
For laughter leads along this way.

## Chasing Phantoms at Dusk

As daylight fades, the phantoms rise,
With mischief twinkling in their eyes.
I chase their whispers, full of glee,
Like bubblegum stuck to a tree.

Each ghostly giggle feels so near,
Yet when I reach, they disappear.
Like socks in laundry, they slip away,
Leaving me puzzled and led astray.

With every step, I trip and fall,
Yet every stumble brings a call.
To dance with shadows, swirl and spin,
In the comical chase, I gleefully grin.

Though clarity's lost in twilight's glow,
My heart is light, my spirit flows.
For in this chase of silly fun,
I find my joy as day is done.

## **The Tangled Webs We Weave**

In a world where socks just disappear,
I search for answers, yet find only fear.
Cats plot and scheme in the dead of night,
While I question if left is ever right.

Lost in the fridge, a mystery loaf,
Is it cake or a science experiment? Oh, woe!
My plants seem to whisper curious things,
I'm a captive in this circus that swings.

The GPS says I'm lost in the park,
How did I get here? I've missed the mark.
Found a way out, or so I believe,
Turns out I'm stuck in a spider's weave!

With laughter and joy, I embrace this mess,
For every confusion, I find happiness.
In tangled webs, I find my delight,
As I dance through chaos, under the light.

## The Diary of a Puzzled Heart

Dear Diary, today I misplaced my shoe,
Wandered the town, not a clue in view.
The barista asked for my name again,
I scribble 'maybe' just to pretend.

My heart skips beats like a broken clock,
Is it love or caffeine? I'll have to mock.
What does the moon whisper when I'm awake?
Is it saying, 'Darling, make me a cake?'

I wear mismatched socks like badges of pride,
Each one a riddle I cannot abide.
To the rhythm of chaos, I skip and twirl,
In this puzzling life, I'll give it a whirl.

With giggles and sighs, I turn each page,
To write my life story, silly and sage.
In the diary of confusion, I see the art,
Of a curious and utterly puzzled heart.

## The Symphony of Unanswered Questions

In the orchestra pit, I fumble and trip,
The conductor is missing, I cling to my grip.
My sheet music's blank, a mistake or a laugh?
The flutes play hiccups as I try to staff.

Is that a tuba or a cat in a box?
The audience chuckles, oh what a paradox!
The trumpets are tooting a grand opera quest,
While I struggle to figure out who's doing best.

Strings begin twanging, a sound so absurd,
Did someone just say 'I like flies in my curds?'
As the concert unfolds in a whimsical haze,
I'm a jester of symphonies caught in a daze.

But laughter erupts like a glorious cheer,
For the melody's chaos brings fondness, oh dear.
In the symphony of questions, I find my way,
To dance with the notes in a quirky ballet.

## **Wandering Through Shadows**

I tiptoe through shadows that twist and sway,
Where do they lead? I'm afraid they may play.
A singing tree hums a tune so bizarre,
But do I trust trees that sport a guitar?

Each petal of night holds a secret so sly,
Why does the moon wink like it's saying hi?
I chase after stars that seem to be fake,
Were they just dreams or a big cosmic prank?

As I pirouette past a two-headed bird,
It squawks out the truth in a language absurd.
Laughter erupts from the shadows I stride,
This silly adventure, I won't try to hide.

With whimsy and joy, I embrace every pause,
In a world filled with wonder, I break all the laws.
Wandering freely, I savor each part,
For life's wild and wacky, a true work of art.

## The Art of Not Knowing

In a world of chaos, I twist and turn,
Trying to grasp what I just couldn't learn.
My brain is a dance floor, all mixed-up beats,
What's left of my thoughts? Just stumbling feats.

Coffee cup emptied, yet still I sit,
Lost in a puzzle, I can't even fit.
Whispers of wisdom, but they all just fade,
Today's confusion is tomorrow's parade.

With each passing second, I lose the plot,
Like socks in the dryer, they vanish a lot.
I nod with a grin, while I'm locked in a trance,
Is it me or the tea that's gone off on a dance?

Life is a circus, I'm holding the string,
But the clown's in charge, and he's lost his ring.
The more I pretend, the less I can see,
An artful confusion, oh, what glee for me!

## Fleeting Thoughts on a Starlit Night

Stars in the sky, they twinkle and laugh,
While I'm here pondering a half-empty glass.
Thoughts zoom around like a comet in flight,
Did I just lose track? Or is it just night?

Moon whispers secrets, while I scratch my head,
What did I come for? Oh, where are my threads?
The dog in the yard now thinks I'm a friend,
But I'm just a stranger, is this where it ends?

Jokes fly like fireflies, they flicker and fade,
All of my questions, they're lost in the shade.
My brain feels like jelly, all wobbly and bright,
What were we talking about? Oh, look! A light!

In silence I wonder, under the vast skies,
Maybe the answers are hidden in pies.
With laughter my guide, I will float in delight,
Fleeting thoughts swirl, oh what a night!

# **Sifting Through Clouds of Meaning**

Caught in the whirlwind of phrases and doubts,
I sift through the clouds, trying to figure it out.
Every sentence I hear, spins round like a wheel,
What makes the most sense? Can someone repeal?

A word here, a phrase there, they drift like the breeze,
Chasing the echoes of unspoken keys.
With quizzical glances, I ponder and pry,
Is there a MapQuest for thoughts in the sky?

Thoughts like confetti, they scatter and twirl,
I'm adrift in a sea of pink ribbons and pearl.
I reach for an anchor, but it slips from my grip,
Navigating nonsense feels like a weird trip.

So here I remain, in this labyrinth vast,
Where answers are shadows, just echoes of past.
But amid the confusion, I chuckle and grin,
What fun is the journey, if chaos can't win?

# Forks in Life's Twisted Road

Here I am standing, at forks in the way,
Should I go left or maybe just sway?
The signs are all blurry, they giggle and tease,
What if the detours just lead to unease?

Maps are for planners, and I've lost my chart,
Hitchhiked to rhythms of a whimsical heart.
With a skip and a hop, I'll dance through the bends,
Embracing the current, my only true friend.

Paths paved with laughter are where I will tread,
With cloud-like confusions swirling in my head.
But thrills in the chaos make me feel alive,
Wandering random, it's how I survive.

So let's raise a toast to the roads that we roam,
Each twist and confusion feels just like a poem.
With humor as currency and joy as my code,
I'll find all the treasures on life's twisted road.

## Waltz of Uncertainty

In a room where socks do hide,
The dance begins, I can't decide.
A step to left, then two to right,
But wait, is that my dog in sight?

Chairs are waltzing, cups may spin,
The chaos here, where do I begin?
A tap on toes, a skip, a slide,
I follow dreams that quickly hide.

A partner leaps from wall to wall,
With every turn, I fear a fall.
The music plays, a tune so strange,
In this ballet, nothing changes.

And yet the laughter fills the air,
With every twist, a goofy stare.
In this absurd, I take my stand,
Embracing moves that feel quite planned.

# **Confusion's Canvas**

Brush in hand, I paint a scene,
With colors bright, but what's it mean?
A splash of blue, a splash of red,
Am I painting? Or just misled?

The canvas laughs, it seems to know,
While I stand puzzled, feeling low.
A sun that's purple, grass that screams,
What a wild world, lost in dreams.

The easel's wobbly, holding tight,
A frowning face stays in my sight.
With every stroke, I start to grin,
As chaos dances with my whim.

In splattered hues, confusion's flair,
I lose myself in creative air.
The art of jest, a funny thing,
In laughter's grasp, I feel the sting.

## Whispers in the Fog

In the mist, I hear them giggle,
A thought comes close, then starts to wiggle.
What did they say? Was it a dare?
Or just a rabbit with fluffy hair?

The trees are bobbing, whisper low,
Secrets hidden, where did they go?
I follow shadows, chase the breeze,
A riddle wrapped with fallen leaves.

Fog swirls thick, it tickles my nose,
A playful spirit that no one knows.
And as I wander, lost in thought,
I sense the aimless fun I sought.

With every turn, the world's a jest,
Where sense and nonsense take their rest.
In the fog, where dreams collide,
Silly whispers become my guide.

# The Dance of Lost Threads

A spool of yarn, it rolls away,
Like thoughts that flee without a say.
I chase it down, but trip and fall,
This dance of threads, it calls us all.

Colors twirling, knots entwine,
A patchwork quilt, mismatched design.
With every tug, confusion grows,
As patterns form, yet no one knows.

A needle pricks, a laugh escapes,
My tangled life in silly shapes.
As I create with threads so loose,
A masterpiece of nonsense, obtuse.

So round and round, the dance will spin,
In threads of chaos, we begin.
It seems the art is not to find,
But celebrate the mixed-up mind.

## **Twists and Turns of Thought**

Every corner I turn is a riddle,
A dance of the mind, oh so little.
Chasing shadows, lost in the twist,
I wave to the sense that I missed.

Maps drawn in crayon, colors collide,
Navigating life with a blindfolded guide.
Thoughts like balloons, they float and they sway,
Which way is up? I have no say.

Jokes in the whispers of each passing breeze,
Tickling my brain with illogical tease.
I trip on the punchline, laugh till I fall,
What was the question? I can't recall.

In the circus of brain's untamed flight,
I juggle my wisdom like fireworks bright.
Pies in the face, with a dash of delight,
Oh, what a clown in this mental fight!

## The Kaleidoscope of Uncertainty


Peering through shards of a glassy design,
Colors collide in a wobbly line.
Shapes twist and turn, creating a scene,
Where nothing is clear, yet all feels serene.

Like socks in the dryer, they spin and they spin,
A chaotic ballet, where does it begin?
Thoughts like marbles, they rattle and roll,
In a wild juggernaut, losing control.

The patterns reshape with a blink and a laugh,
As I chase vague echoes on my silly path.
Each tap of my toe feels like a surprise,
What's hiding behind these bewildered skies?

With every new twist, the laughter unfurls,
Life's a confetti of swirling twirls.
I'll dance in confusion, no map in my hand,
Embracing this wonder, oh isn't it grand?

## **A Song of Hesitation**

I tiptoe through feelings that rise and fall,
A waltz on the edge, will I drop? Not at all!
Questions like bubbles, they float in my mind,
Pop! There goes logic, I leave it behind.

Wobbling words on this merry-go-round,
Do I smile, do I frown? What's to be found?
Just when I think I might grasp a clue,
The floorboards are creaking, adieu to my view.

In the hall of mirrors, I laugh at my grace,
Reflections are guffaws in this quirky space.
With each turn I take, I'm less and less sure,
But oh! What a tune this uncertainty's pure.

Strung between moments that giggle and sway,
I'll dance in the limbo of this odd ballet.
Every hesitated step brings joy to the song,
In this wacky world where nothing feels wrong!

**Conundrums at Dusk**

As day dips low, and shadows grow tall,
Pondering mysteries, I stumble and sprawl.
The sky paints puzzles in colors so bold,
Yet answers stay hidden, wrapped up and cold.

Whispers of nonsense on the evening breeze,
Questioning snacks, or the mysteries of cheese?
The flicker of stars just adds to the jest,
Are they winking at me? Or is it a test?

Time slips away like a cat in a sun,
Chasing my thoughts but can't seem to run.
Each quirk of the dusk brings giggles and sighs,
In a world full of questions, I'm searching for pies.

Twists in the twilight, so funny and bright,
Where laughter and wonder take flight in the night.
With each silly query that pops in my head,
I find joy in confusion, much fun instead!

## The Architecture of Confusion


In a house where doors lead nowhere,
And windows show a painted sky,
The floor plans seem to lose their flair,
I trip on thoughts that zoom and fly.

There's a sign that says 'Turn Left,' but it's
A right turn that led me astray,
I'm lost in this maze of funny hits,
Where reason plays a game of delay.

The walls whisper secrets, oh so sly,
Chasing cats that dance on the floor,
While echoes of laughter amplify,
Questions chase me out the door.

Blueprints chart confusion's terrain,
With architects who lost their minds,
Yet in this chaos, there's no pain,
Just laughter wrapped in tangled lines.

## Clocks That Don't Tick

Waking up to a sun that's shy,
The clocks are all set to undefined,
Time sips coffee, waves goodbye,
While I'm just here, unaligned.

The seconds zigzag in merry loops,
As minutes go on a brunch date,
I'm left with thoughts, tangled groups,
Questions swirl like a plate of fate.

I counted sheep, but they sold out,
For answers, I'm still in the queue,
Each tick that doesn't is a shout,
Telling me, 'You've got no clue.'

So here I sip my cloudy tea,
Wrapped in a blanket of jest,
Life's a riddle, come laugh with me,
In this timeless, quirky quest.

## The Shadow of Doubt

In the garden where flowers wilt,
A shadow dances, tall and sly,
It giggles at the mess we built,
And nods like it knows why.

With whispers that tickle my ear,
It plants ideas, seeds of fun,
While I'm flailing, gripped by fear,
As if I forgot how to run.

It knows my worries like a friend,
And plays tricks with my tangled mind,
A jester wearing doubt's latest trend,
Hiding wisdom one can't find.

So let's embrace this playful game,
Invite confusion to the jest,
For in this shadow, there's no shame,
Just laughter in the wild quest.

**Eclipsed by Questions**

The moon hides behind a veil of haze,
As worries circle, round and round,
In a dance of confusing ways,
Where answers just can't be found.

With each query, stars start to fade,
And logic takes a little break,
In this cosmic, star-studded parade,
I seek the answers I won't bake.

A comet zips, trails questions bright,
Across the sky of my bewildered brain,
Here in the dark, I find my light,
As I laugh through this silly reign.

Questions play tag with no escape,
But I'll frolic on this cosmic shore,
For even in this baffling landscape,
Every giggle opens more and more.

## The Chasm of Indecision

I stand between two doors so bright,
Which one to choose? I lost my sight.
The left one sings a silly tune,
The right one dances with a spoon.

Confusion wraps like a fuzzy scarf,
My brain's a circus, oh what a laugh!
Logic waves a tiny flag,
As I fumble like a bumbling hag.

I trip on thoughts that twist and shout,
Every option wrapped in doubt.
Like a penguin on a skateboard,
I wobble, teeter, and then I'm floored.

Maybe it's time to bring a snack,
Forget the path, just take a crack.
A pie in hand, decisions fade,
I guess I'll just enjoy the parade.

## Whispers of Confounding Times

The clock ticks back, then forward too,
What time is it? I haven't a clue!
The cat is plotting, or so it seems,
While I chase shadows in my dreams.

A knock upon the door resounds,
Is it a friend or a lost hound?
The leaves are chatting in the breeze,
I nod along, oh yes, with ease!

Questions bounce like rubber balls,
Each one weird, like funny calls.
Do I wear socks? Should I wear shoes?
I'll take both! Who can refuse?

Every moment is a joyful riddle,
Twisting thoughts—just like a fiddle.
With laughter echoing all around,
I dance through life, forever unbound.

# A Map with No Directions

I hold a map, but it's upside down,
Where I'm headed? I wear a frown.
The X marks a spot that's way off track,
I'm just a traveler with a snack pack.

The compass spins as if in a whirl,
North, south, east—ah, give it a twirl!
I'll ask that penguin with a top hat,
"Excuse me, sir, which way to that?"

Signposts hold hands in a silent fight,
Pointing left while I think right.
But giggles echo from every turn,
Who knew that wrong could feel so learned?

With jumbled thoughts and a chart of stars,
I'll find my way past Venus and Mars.
Destination's just a quirky game,
And getting lost just adds to the fame.

## Contradictions in Every Corner

In one hand candy, in the other, greens,
My diet's a puzzle of comical scenes.
Maybe I'll bake a shoe-shaped pie,
Just to see how high I can fly!

I tell myself to rise and grind,
While cozy blankets pull me behind.
Maybe tomorrow, I'll take a jog,
But for now, let's nap like a hog.

I scream that I'll take the scenic route,
But end up lost, not even cute.
Each twist and turn a brand new laugh,
Oh, what a weird and wobbly path!

The world offers options, wild and vast,
But I just giggle; this too shall pass.
With contradictions wrapped tight like a bow,
I'll twirl through life, just going with the flow.

## Wandering Without a Map

With my compass pointing south,
I laugh at the twists I take.
Every turn leads to a sigh,
As I ponder the route I make.

Clouds above play tricks on me,
They shift like thoughts in a stew.
The signs all point to nowhere,
And I'm lost, but what's new?

A dog barks at a squirrel,
As I trip over my own two feet.
The world's a giant puzzle,
And I can't find a single piece.

Yet laughter fills the spaces,
Where confusion joins the fun.
In this wacky, wild journey,
I think I've only just begun.

## **Confusion's Dance**

Spin me round, I'm on a spree,
Twisting paths like spaghetti.
Each step a leap into the unknown,
With rhythm so fast, I'm not alone.

A cat meows, the clock strikes ten,
What's the time? I count to ten.
The floor feels like it's not quite there,
And should I really stop and stare?

Laughter bubbles, a quirky tune,
As shadows shimmy under the moon.
Who is leading this silly dance?
I shrug it off, let's take a chance.

In the chaos, we find our grace,
With every stumble, our silly face.
A jig of joy, a skip of fate,
In confusion's dance, we all relate.

## An Odyssey of Doubt

Off I go, into the blue,
With mismatched socks and wrong shoes.
My map is crumpled, my mind a blur,
Where I'm headed? I'm not quite sure.

The road forks left, then twists and bends,
Bumping into invisible friends.
Each conversation makes less sense,
Like jokes wrapped in a dense pretense.

A signpost blinks, 'Do not enter',
But it looks like a fun adventure.
So with a chuckle, I march right in,
Who knew chaos could feel like a win?

With coffee stains and silly hats,
My heart is light, despite the spats.
In this odyssey of dazzling doubt,
The journey matters, not the route.

## Fragments of a Fading Mind

Fragments scatter like confetti,
Thoughts drift slow, oh so heady.
A puzzle box without a key,
My brain's a circus, can you see?

Juggling ideas, they fall and break,
Each one whispers, 'What's at stake?'
Stored away in disarray,
Colors blur at the end of the day.

Words escape like bubbles in air,
I reach, but find none anywhere.
Once clear thoughts now fuzzy lines,
A quirky dance of tangled signs.

Yet here I chuckle, through the haze,
Finding joy in this tangled maze.
For in fragments, life's essence shines,
And laughter unlocks the tightest minds.

## The Labyrinth of Mind's Eye

In the maze of thoughts I roam,
Chasing shadows, far from home.
Left turns lead me to a wall,
Guess I'll bounce and risk a fall.

Maps I drew are upside down,
Every turn, I wear a frown.
With each corner, new surprise,
Is that a door, or just skies?

Overthinking's quite an art,
Every riddle breaks my heart.
Logic's lost, in swirling haze,
Help! I'm trapped in this mind maze!

Maybe I should just unwind,
Forget the route and be unkind.
To every thought that makes me dance,
Embrace the chaos, take a chance!

## Watching Clouds Play Hide and Seek

Clouds above, so soft and light,
Hiding, peeking, what a sight!
One's a bunny, then a shoe,
What are they? I haven't a clue.

Chasing them is quite a game,
Lost and found, it's all the same.
Do they laugh when they disappear?
Or just float off without a care?

Sky's a canvas, blue and pure,
But clouds, oh how they love to lure.
One minute here, next gone away,
Like my thoughts on a cloudy day!

I'll just sit and watch their play,
As they drift and sway all day.
In this game of hide and seek,
I seek sense, but they are sleek!

## Conversations with a Blank Slate

A blank page asks me what to write,
I shrug my shoulders, won't ignite.
It stares back with a gentle grin,
Maybe this chat's where I begin!

What do you think? Another idea?
The silence whispers, 'Change the gear.'
I toss around some fickle dreams,
But all I hear are muted screams.

I scribble thoughts, they fade away,
Like echoes from a distant play.
The slate just giggles, 'Try again!'
I laugh back, 'This could be our zen!'

So I chat with this empty space,
Finding comfort in its embrace.
In the nonsense, we find a groove,
Two clowns in the dark, making a move!

# The Enigma of Everyday


Woke up today, where's my shoe?
The kitchen's gone, what's wrong with you?
Breakfast whispers, 'What's your plan?'
I point and nod, like some madman.

Coffee spills like morning rain,
I laugh it off, embrace the strain.
The toast is dancing, please don't burn,
To chaos and crumbs, I now return!

The cat is plotting something grand,
While missing my keys, I search the land.
The fridge hums low, a secret tune,
I'm convinced it's plotting, oh what a boon!

Maybe today will lead to cheer,
In everyday whimsy, I have no fear.
With laughter and joy, I'll twist and twirl,
As the world spins, my thoughts unfurl!

## Shadows of the Unknown

In a room that's filled with chatter,
I sit and wonder, what's the matter?
My coffee's cold, my mind's a blur,
    Is that a cat or just a fur?

The clock ticks on, what does it mean?
I lost my phone, or was it seen?
I wave at strangers, is that wrong?
    They wave back; I hum along.

The fridge hums low, a friendly tune,
Did I just hear a talking spoon?
I shake my head and laugh aloud,
    In my chaos, I'm so proud!

Every shadow whispers sweet,
Of jokes and tales I can't repeat.
I skip on clouds, I dance in mist,
    In my puzzle, I still persist.

## The Jigsaw of Life


Pieces scattered, no edge in sight,
Is this a puzzle or a kite?
I find a piece that's bright and bold,
But it's a shoe—what's the hold?

With colors clashing, joy in my stride,
Maybe it's just a foolish ride.
They say it's fun; I can't quite see,
Why life's a game, but not for me.

I push and poke at every bit,
Is that a corner? What's a fit?
With every laugh, a sigh escapes,
I draw more symbols than shapes.

A picture forms that's out of whack,
A duck on fire, or is it black?
Yet here I am with jest and cheer,
In my jigsaw, I persevere!

## Unraveled Thoughts

I woke this morning, thought I'd try,
To knit my brain, oh me, oh my!
The yarn got tangled, made a mess,
Guess I'm a poet in distress.

Ideas run like cats at play,
I chase them down, they slip away.
A sock for warmth, a hat for style,
But all I'm left with is a smile.

What color? What pattern? Who can say?
My scarf's a tiger, my thoughts at bay.
I trip on threads, I dance in glee,
Lost in the whims of make-believe.

Yet in this snarl, I find delight,
Each tangled thought is pure insight.
With giggles ringing, I'll wear my art,
In chaos, friend, you'll find your heart.

## When Clarity Takes a Vacation

The sun is bright, the sky's a show,
But where's my brain? I just don't know.
With ice cream drips and laughter shared,
I search for sense, but none is spared.

A map I made, without a rhyme,
Leads to nowhere, but it's just fine.
I take a turn, I lose my way,
Is this the price I have to pay?

Conversations buzz like bees in flight,
I nod along; it feels so right.
But as the world spins round and round,
What's lost is magic, not profound.

So here I sit, with blissful grin,
In this wild ride, I'll take a spin.
With clarity gone, I won't despair,
In mystery's arms, I find my flair!

## Signs Written in Invisible Ink

I found a map, all covered in stains,
X marks the spot, but it's full of refrains.
Directions unclear, like a cat in a tree,
I'm lost in the mystery of what could be.

The guide is a penguin in a top hat,
He points to the sky while I'm stuck on the mat.
With chicken scratch notes and arrows that bend,
It's a circus of chaos that has no end.

A compass that spins like a disco ball,
I'm trying to dance but I'm tripping and fall.
The signs are all foggy, the words disappear,
I'm laughing so hard, it's all just so clear.

I take a wrong turn and follow a bee,
It leads me to nowhere, as fun as can be.
I'll follow this path till I run out of snacks,
In a land full of nonsense, my sanity cracks.

## The Colors of a Tangled Mind

A rainbow of thoughts is stuck in my head,
Each color a question, with answers unsaid.
Red is for madness, blue's for the chill,
While green's for the vibes that are hard to distill.

Mixing it up like a painter gone wild,
The hues drip together, it's chaos compiled.
I wander through fields of polka dot skies,
Searching for meaning in gumdrops and lies.

The yellow's too bright, it gives me a fright,
Like a clown in the corner, lurking at night.
Orange whispers secrets I have yet to learn,
In a kaleidoscope dance, I still feel the churn.

With each stroke of thought, I paint a new scene,
Laughter erupts when it's silly or mean.
My tangled creations, a puzzle to see,
A canvas of nonsense, it's perfect to me.

## Scribbles in the Margin of Reality

Margins are filled with doodles and quirks,
Where sanity flutters and madness unworks.
I scribble some notes that don't make any sense,
It's a wild ride of thought, no need for pretense.

A unicorn's walking my dog on a leash,
They dance past the coffee that bubbles like Greece.
Symbols and arrows lead nowhere at all,
A scribble in ink that bends into a sprawl.

The pages are cluttered with hopes and with fears,
Tickle the dragon, it laughs and it sneers.
Each line is a riddle, each squiggle's a dream,
In the margin of life, nothing's as it seems.

Bubbles and squiggles lead down a black hole,
Where thinking is silly; it's good for the soul.
In the margins I linger, with whimsy in sight,
Reality's edges are blurry and bright.

## Chasing Shadows on a Moonlit Path

Under the moon, shadows twist and they twirl,
A dance that is quirky in a magical whirl.
I follow their lead, though I'm really not sure,
If the path is just silly or something much more.

The trees play hide-and-seek, whispering low,
As fireflies chuckle, they steal the show.
My shoes are on backward; my hat's on the ground,
This jest of a journey is profoundly unbound.

A rabbit in spectacles points to the stars,
With riddles to solve that are dressed up in bars.
I leap when they vanish, I chase after light,
In the chase of the shadows, I'm feeling just right.

A giggle escapes from the soft, blooming night,
With questions like bubbles that float out of sight.
In this whimsical chase, I find joy in the run,
For the laughter of shadows is always such fun.

## The Curious Case of Ambiguity

In a room full of hats, I wear just a shoe,
The cat reads the news, and I'm lost in the stew.
What's baked in the oven? A mystery divine,
While squirrels debate if the sun is a sign.

The clock makes a noise like a duck with a cold,
And whispers of planets in colors untold.
Should I dance with the fridge or chat with the floor?
A tango with shadows, now that's an encore!

A sandwich speaks French, then shouts out a tune,
The toaster's a bard with tales of the moon.
I trip over thoughts that swirl out of reach,
Words play hide and seek, but they never would teach.

In the circus of nonsense, I'm front-row tonight,
With popcorn in hand, and the world's gone awright.
So let's toast to the quirks and embrace the parade,
For life's just a dance that's sweetly delayed.

## The Void Between Whispers


A butterfly whispered to a sneaky old chair,
While tacos debated the art of a stare.
The moon took a nap; it was pillow-fort time,
As clouds played the trumpet, creating a rhyme.

I tried to have tea with a well-dressed spoon,
But it chose to waltz with a lounge-loving moon.
What's happening here? Is all lost in the breeze?
I ask a goldfish; it beckons with ease.

Every tick of the clock is a riddle, you see,
As I tie my shoe laces to strands of a tree.
The stars are good listeners, or so they once said,
But tonight they are busy with dancing instead.

So I'll scribble my thoughts on a paper-thin breeze,
And hug every moment, with chuckles and ease.
For life is a puzzle that giggles and waits,
In the void of confusion, we dance like in states.

## Meandering Through a Maze

In a labyrinth wide where the walls wear a grin,
I chase after echoes of where to begin.
A snail writes a novel in letters of slime,
While I ponder the meaning of blueberries and crime.

Around every corner, a pancake rolls by,
Wearing syrupy goggles, oh my, how they fly!
I wave at the hedgehogs, they wink and take flight,
My map is a doodle, it's all black and white.

The cheese stands alone; it has much to impart,
In whispers of dreams that are lost in the tart.
Where's the exit sign? I cannot quite tell,
As marshmallows giggle and set off a spell.

So hop on a cloud and chase laughter instead,
In a maze of confetti, where giggles are fed.
For wandering's wisdom is strewn with delight,
And every wrong turn is a bird in a flight.

## A Symphony of Misunderstandings

A trumpet played salsa to a knock on the door,
While biscuits debated if they should encore.
The piano was tickling a bunch of ripe pears,
As shadows performed in their fanciful lairs.

A symphony started with a sneeze from a cat,
Encouraging flowers to dance in a hat.
The violin shouted a song made of cheese,
As everyone chuckled at secrets like these.

Flamingos wore ties to the concert of dreams,
Where jellybeans played with the moon's silver beams.
The beat of confusion wrapped round like a hug,
With rhythms that made all the nonsense seem snug.

So we danced all night on the notes of despair,
With giggles and rhythms that floated in air.
For life is a tune with a twist and a turn,
In the symphony's chaos, we all take our turn.

# Entangled in Thoughts

In a world of swirling dreams,
I chase my thoughts like cats in beams.
They leap and pounce without a care,
Leaving me lost in frantic air.

With every turn, there's rabbit holes,
And I'm just searching for my goals.
But all I find are socks and shoes,
And memes that leave me with the blues.

I try to focus, gather brawn,
But the laundry's calling me at dawn.
So I sit, perplexed, and have a snack,
As my brain gives up, and starts to crack.

Oh, what a mess is in my mind,
With chaos true, and peace hard to find.
I laugh aloud at this wild spree,
As I embrace this quirky glee.

# The Weight of Uncertainty

I walked outside, but lost my keys,
The squirrels laugh, they're such a tease.
The clouds, they change from gray to white,
I ponder if it's day or night.

I tried to bake a simple pie,
But ended up with a fruit stir-fry.
The recipe's a mystery, oh dear,
I overcooked my hopes, I fear.

The map I read has words I know,
But where to turn? I just don't flow.
Directions given make me frown,
As I wander further from the town.

I carry this weight of what could be,
While giggling at the folly of me.
With every step, a twist unfolds,
In this circus life, I have been sold.

## Dreams of Clarity

I dreamt of answers, clear as day,
But woke to chaos and dismay.
The moon conspired with my brain,
And left me here, all sunk in rain.

The coffee brews, it steams and swirls,
I question life with dizzy twirls.
What's the meaning? Where's the zest?
I laugh at fate, it's such a jest.

Should I wear socks with sandals bright?
This ponder makes me laugh outright.
I'll dance through mishaps, twirl with glee,
While wondering what the world could be.

The dreams of clarity, they come and go,
Like ice cream melted in the flow.
A sprinkle here, a waffle there,
Life's silly truth—who really cares?

## The Unfolding Paradox


There's logic here, or is it wrong?
I sing a silly, off-key song.
Each paradox begins to bloom,
As I dance around the vacuum.

Invisible forces pull and tug,
I stub my toe on an old rug.
With every twist, I laugh and grin,
At baffling truths, where do I begin?

I ponder deeply with my toast,
Are constants real, or just a boast?
The kettle whistles, screaming loud,
While I'm entranced by thoughts uncowed.

The world unfolds in wondrous ways,
With all its quirks, and fray and craze.
In laughter's arms, I'll take a stand,
In this bizarre, absurd land.

## The Enigma of Everyday Life

I woke up this morning, thought I was late,
Pajamas on backwards, that's just my fate.
Coffee in the toaster, a cat in the sink,
Trying to ponder, what am I missing, I think?

The clock's running fast, or is it too slow?
I tripped on my thoughts, now where did they go?
Keys in the fridge, and my phone's in the car,
Living like this, I'm a strange little star.

Words on my tongue, but they don't want to talk,
I'm walking the dog, but it's me who will walk.
Chasing my shadow, or is it the sun?
Guess I'll keep running, this race isn't done.

With laughter in chaos, I'll take on the day,
When nothing makes sense, let's giggle away.
So here's to the puzzles, let's dance in delight,
Embracing the wacky, oh what a sight!

## Navigating the Grey

I put on my shoes, found one's a bit wet,
Sunshine or rain? I've no clue yet.
Maps in my pocket, but no place to go,
Asking directions from a friendly stow.

The sky is a canvas; is that blue or grey?
My mind's in the cloud, what was I to say?
Driving in circles, roundabouts and fear,
Each turn a new riddle, oh where's the clear?

Puzzles on paper, yet none have a key,
I'm lost in the shades of what could be me.
Laughter and giggles, in the fog I shall roam,
Finding my way through this glorious dome.

Every step's a riddle, each pause a delight,
With friends by my side, we'll dance through the night.
So here's to uncertainty, cheers all around,
Let's wade through the grey with laughter unbound!

## The Soundtrack of Confusion

Coffee brews loudly, like it's in a fight,
My cereal's dancing, oh what a sight!
Lost in a melody that goes out of tune,
What's that? I mused, a cow or a balloon?

Tunes from the weather, swaying leaves in a breeze,
My cat has a solo, oh please, oh please!
The radio buzzes, it's news or a song,
In the chorus of chaos, I can't help but throng.

The blender's a drummer, my phone rings a bell,
Echoes of laughter, oh can't you tell?
Each note's a humor wrapped up in a jest,
Finding the rhythm, we will jest with zest.

So turn up the volume, let's dance with the sound,
For in the confusion, true joy can be found.
A symphony's flashing, let's dance all night,
In comical serenades, we'll take flight!

## In the Heart of Ambivalence

Should I grab the umbrella, or just wear a grin?
Weather's a mystery, let the games begin.
Decisions like puzzles, where'd I drop the piece?
In the heart of ambivalence, I seek my release.

Flip a coin? Or just flip-flop instead?
I might wear odd socks, who's keeping me fed?
In a world of choices, my brain's on the flop,
Either way, I'll savor this vivacious hop.

A dance on the fence, I'm ne'er feeling blue,
For every 'yes' leads to a funky 'no' too.
Embracing the chaos, and throwing confetti,
In the heart of the mix, life's whims are so petty.

So here's to the laughter, the fun quandaries bring,
In the swirl of confusion, let's jump and sing.
ith friends and good vibes, let the swirling commence,
For in ambivalence, it all makes sense!

## The Unwritten Chapters

In a world of scattered pages,
Mysteries dance in quirky stages.
Puzzles jigsaw with missing parts,
Laughter bubbles in strange hearts.

Plot twists hide in cereal bowls,
Lost socks preach to wandering souls.
Each chapter ends, but what comes next?
A comedy of chaos, quite perplexed.

Do we scribble stories or just doodle?
Heroes come with unplayed poodle.
The narrators are confused as well,
In this tale where laughter swells.

Scribbles and giggles, a wild array,
Waiting for fortune or mishap's play.
In unwritten chapters, we might find,
The joy of nonsense—oh, so kind!

## Navigating the Unknown

A compass spins like a ballerina,
Pointing to places like a can of tuna.
Maps are doodles by someone who's lost,
The thrill is fun, regardless of cost.

Wanderers trip over their own two feet,
Chasing shadows, though none are neat.
The guidebook wrote itself a joke,
Each detour adds spice, that's the poke!

Sailing skies of uncharted air,
Finding treasures in socks laid bare.
Every wrong turn is a chance for cheer,
Embrace the folly, there's nothing to fear.

So let's set sail on this quirky spree,
With flares of laughter, we'll simply be.
In the unknown, there's glee to share,
Maps are funnier when none are there!

## In the Thicket of Thoughts

Thoughts entwine like tangled vines,
Lost in daydreams, where humor shines.
Ideas sprout like weeds of doubt,
Swirling questions, roundabout.

Whispers giggle beneath the trees,
Squirrels plan a grand comedy tease.
Do we dive deep or just float around?
In this thicket, silliness is found.

Each idea tiptoes, searching for bliss,
Every chance taken, a laugh we miss.
Gravity pulls the wittiest guys,
In the thicket, the prankster flies.

So we navigate chaos with a grin,
Wondering where dreams might begin.
In this mess of thoughts and dreams,
The humor's there, or so it seems!

## The Allure of Uncertainty


What's that noise? A tumble or shout?
A sudden thrill—what's that about?
Life sends puzzles that spark delight,
In the dance of chance, we take flight.

Easter eggs hide, oh what a prank!
Finding answers in the midst of dank.
Every mishap's a reason to cheer,
In uncertainty, we lose all fear.

The lure of 'maybe' speaks in rhyme,
Tickling fancies, biding our time.
We juggle the odd with a cheeky grin,
With each twist of fate, we jump right in.

So come join the riddle, the funny parade,
In the allure of chance, we've got it made.
No crystal balls or foresight divine,
In this odd circus, we're all just fine!

## **Frayed Edges of Reality**

Woke up this morning, socks don't match,
Coffee's in the toaster, what a catch!
Maps upside down, is this a trick?
Guess I'll just dance, it sounds like a kick.

My phone's a banana, I call it lunch,
The cat's in charge, giving orders to munch.
Reality's jigsaw, pieces scattered wide,
Maybe it's best just to enjoy the ride.

Questions fill my head, but answers are shy,
Like trying to catch a cloud passing by.
Laughing at nonsense, my favorite game,
In this wild circus, we're all just the same.

So I spin in my chair, throw caution with glee,
In this strange dance of life, come twirl with me!
Frayed edges wiggle, colors bleed bright,
Let's celebrate chaos, it feels just right.

## **In Search of the Obvious**

Lost in a forest of thoughts in my head,
The obvious path is not what I tread.
I'm hunting for answers, a treasure that's rare,
But all I encounter is the sound of thin air.

Turn left at confusion, go right through the haze,
I'm gazing at signs that all seem to maze.
A cookie for wisdom, forgot where it's stored,
Mysterious crumbs make me feel quite adored.

Every clue leads to giggles and sighs,
Maybe the answers wear bright, silly ties.
But it's all so elusive, like mist in the sun,
The quest for the obvious, oh what a fun run!

So, I chase my own tail, in circles I spin,
Where did I put that? Oh where to begin?
With laughter as my compass, I wander and roam,
In search of the obvious, I've found my home.

## Labyrinthine Musings

In a maze made of thoughts, I walk with a grin,
Each turn brings a chuckle, confusion my kin.
Right might mean left, contradictions galore,
Like opening a window that leads to a door.

I tried to measure thoughts, but they're slippery fish,
Caught in wild tangles, twirling in dish.
Sketching in circles, like art gone awry,
The deeper I go, the more I just fly.

Thought bubbles pop, they dance and they swim,
Ideas like noodles, they stretch and they brim.
Round and around, on this rollercoaster ride,
Laughter my anchor, through the swirling tide.

So here's to the puzzles that baffle the wise,
In the realm of the wacky, we're all on the rise.
With joy as our treasure, let's play hide and seek,
In labyrinthine musings, it's fun to be weak!

## The Surrender to the Unknown

Throw in the towel, let's take a deep breath,
Navigating life feels like a game of chess.
My knight's gone missing, queen's sipping tea,
The board is a mess, who's winning? Not me!

I'll toss out the map, let's turn off the lights,
With giggles and stumbles, we'll ignite the nights.
Follow the breadcrumbs, but wait, where'd they go?
I'll just eat the bread, let my tummy know.

The fog's my best friend, wraps me in glee,
In this dance of the silly, I'm wild and free.
Plans made of jelly, ideas in bloom,
Who needs a schedule when chaos can zoom?

So cheers to uncertainty, the spark of the show,
With laughter as my guide, let's dive into the flow.
Hand in hand we'll frolic, through paths yet untold,
In surrender to the unknown, let's be brave and bold!

## The Labyrinth of Questions

In a maze of thoughts I roam,
What's that? A cat or a gnome?
Twists and turns lead me astray,
Do I even know the day?

Maps are useless, fun to fold,
Advice from a crystal, often cold.
Left or right? Oh what a game!
They all look the same, oh what a shame!

A door of socks, a window of cheese,
Caught in riddles that don't appease.
Should I laugh or should I cry?
Wait—who's that sneaking by?

Puzzles dance in the air,
Why's that banana on a chair?
Questions tumble, no answers near,
Yet here I giggle, full of cheer!

## Echoes in the Darkness

In the shadows, whispers sing,
Do they mean what they bring?
Tick tock, but time stands still,
Is that a ghost or just my will?

Footsteps flutter, bounce around,
Are they lost, or homeward bound?
Lights flicker, mood is spry,
Catch a glimpse, oh what a high!

Boo! Is that your face?
Or just me in this odd place?
Laughter echoes in the gloom,
Masked in shimmering, silly bloom.

Hiding secrets, shadows sprout,
What's it all about, no doubt?
With a grin that splits the dark,
It's an adventure, let's embark!

## The Colors of Ambiguity

Is this red or is it blue?
Maybe green? Oh, who knew!
Colors swirl in cups of tea,
What on earth could this all be?

Graffiti thoughts paint the air,
A zebra with a funky pair.
Am I seeing upside down?
Or did my brain just take a crown?

Brush strokes tickle, shapes abound,
A polka-dotted square is found.
Is that a smile or a pout?
Confusion reigns, there's no doubt!

Rainbow giggles burst in flight,
Colors shimmer, what a sight!
In this canvas of delight,
Let's dance away into the night!

## Sailing on a Sea of Mystery

A boat made of paper, or so it seems,
Drifting through a sea of dreams.
Waves of giggles splash around,
What treasure waits to be found?

Captain of chaos, am I the one?
Or just the jester having fun?
Anchors weigh less than my thought,
Where's the map? Oh, I forgot!

Seagulls squawk in riddled tones,
Are they calling me, or are they clones?
Stars above twinkle with glee,
Should I steer left, or let it be?

In this ship, we spin and twirl,
Lost in waves that twist and whirl.
The horizon laughs, a grand display,
Join the dance, come what may!

## Mists of Misunderstanding

In a world of twists and turns,
I seek to catch the clues.
With every step, the lesson burns,
Yet I'm still reading news.

Things spinning like a dizzy top,
The answers flee like ghosts.
I'd love a map, but then I'd stop,
And ponder questions most.

I asked a cat for wisdom rare,
It just stared back, bemused.
The puzzle grows, I pull my hair,
As sanity's confused.

A parade of socks and mismatched shoes,
Walks past my foggy sight.
They know the dance, I've got the blues,
In this ridiculous night.

## Labors of a Bewildered Heart

With a wink and a nod, I try to play,
At love's ridiculous game.
But every turn leads me astray,
And I'm caught in someone's frame.

I set my sights on dinner plans,
Yet ended at a zoo.
Amongst the bears and monkey bands,
My heart says, "This feels new!"

The chocolate cake was quite a treat,
But the mess? A grand affair.
I've wrestled with my own two feet,
And still have more to share.

With each blunder, I charm the day,
While laughter's my disguise.
In this wild and silly ballet,
I just hope to win the prize.

## Uncharted Waters

In the boat of life, I drift and sway,
No compass to call my own.
The stars, they wink, then fade away,
Leaving me here alone.

I ask a fish which way to go,
It twirls and swims in glee.
Each splash a riddle, don't you know,
It's cryptic fishy poetry.

The waves whisper secrets in my ear,
But all I hear is 'blub.'
My hopes, they rise, but then they veer,
Like popcorn in a tub.

So, here I float in swirling night,
With giggles and a sigh.
Adrift in chaos, blind to light,
I'll laugh until I cry.

## The Riddles of Existence

At the intersections of my thoughts,
A traffic jam of fun.
I ponder why, when all is fraught,
I end up on the run.

With fortune cookies in my hand,
I read their cryptic notes.
One said 'Unravel each demand,'
I guess I'll buy some coats.

When life gives options—left or right,
I'll just try to dance.
With silly steps, I'll feel just right,
In this chaotic trance.

So here's to all the silly jests,
And laughter found at dawn.
For in this life, though all feels jest,
We'll sing until it's gone.

## Unsung Questions

Why is the sky a vast blue dome?
Does it ever feel lonely, far from home?
The cat keeps staring at the wall,
Is it plotting? Or just having a ball?

What's in the fridge? A science fair?
Leftovers? Mystery soup? I don't dare!
Why do socks vanish without a trace?
Did they join a circus? Or a space race?

Why do ducks waddle, looking so cool?
Are they the wise ones, playing the fool?
Do plants ever gossip when we're away?
Or just sit in silence, growing each day?

Oh, the riddles tumble, a joyful mess,
In the theater of life, we must confess.
Each question lingers, tickling the mind,
And in the laughter, the answers we find.

## **The Circus of Unknowing**

Step right up to the show of the year!
Clowns juggle questions, diverse and queer.
Why does popcorn hop in the pan?
Is it just trying to be a food fan?

Tigers roam free with puzzled looks,
As if they've read some baffling books.
Why do we dance when there's no beat?
Is our sanity on a perpetual heat?

The strongman lifts weights made of air,
While the tightrope walker is not even there.
What's the meaning behind a goldfish's stare?
In this circus of thoughts, we're all in despair.

But laughter erupts, the audience bright,
With questions that vanish into the night.
In a world full of wild, perplexing play,
We find our joy in the silliness of the day.

## A Mind Like a Maze

A twist and a turn, where am I now?
Did I stray from the cake or the cow?
With thoughts like a maze, I wander about,
Trying to escape, but there's no way out.

Every corner hides a curious sight,
Like sock puppets hosting a midnight fight.
If I turn the right way, will I find the cheese?
Or just run into another baffling tease?

I chase my own tail, like a dog on a quest,
Wondering if this wandering's truly the best.
Is that a rabbit wearing a fancy hat?
Or just my imagination playing with that?

At the end of this maze, what do I find?
A jumble of giggles, all intertwined.
So come join this journey, it's sure to amuse,
In the labyrinth of life, we've nothing to lose.

## Reflections in a Distorted Mirror

In the mirror, I see a face quite strange,
A hodgepodge of features that seem to change.
Why do I laugh at my own silly grin?
Is that the reflection of where I've been?

Each angle reveals a new quirky sight,
Like fish wearing hats in broad daylight.
Do shadows ever trip on their own feet?
Or is that just my mind's own shuffle beat?

Echoes of thoughts bounce off the glass,
A strange little dance, a glorious class.
Is that a unicorn lurking behind?
Or just the remnants of dreams left behind?

In the land of distortions, we all are free,
To ponder the nonsense, oh woe is me!
But laughter rings out, sharp and sincere,
In these reflections, let's hold dear.

## Echoes of the Unsure

In a room full of laughter, I grin with a sigh,
Thoughts bouncing like marbles, oh me, oh my.
Questions whirl like a dance, in a dizzying spin,
What's that little noise? Let the fun begin!

I wear mismatched socks, is this the right shoe?
Maps made of candy, are they meant for the zoo?
A parrot on my shoulder just told me to wait,
Should I trust his advice or just savor my fate?

The calendar's blank, it's a day of delight,
When will the sun rise? Is it morning or night?
The cookies are burnt, I'm not sure how it's done,
But hey, it's a party; let's all just have fun!

Juggling with questions, I'm a clown in the dark,
Bright ideas are flying like a question mark.
With each silly wink, and a nod of my head,
I'm diving in laughter; who needs to be fed?

## Tidal Waves of What If

What if the cat talks, but we just can't hear?
What if the clouds are made of cotton candy, my dear?
I sit on the shore watching waves come and go,
Riding on tides of confusion, just letting it flow.

A fish waves hello, does he know what I think?
My coffee cup whispers, 'Time for a drink!'
Curious thoughts float like balloons in the sky,
Chasing after dreams, wondering how and why.

What if the stars all come down to play?
A game of hopscotch, under the moon's sway.
I'm counting in circles; it feels like a race,
With socks on my hands, my own little space.

Laughter erupts as the clock strikes a tune,
A dance in the living room, how silly, how soon!
Questions like seafoam, just drift and just roll,
In waves of the whimsical, I'm lost in my soul.

# Forgotten Maps in the Attic

Dusty old dreams lie beneath the old beams,
Maps full of treasures and whimsical themes.
Directions to nowhere, with arrows that spin,
Leading me places where nonsense begins.

A compass that giggles, it points to my shoes,
The attic is buzzing with giggles and blues.
Is that a lost sock? Oh wait, is it two?
Mysterious artifacts, what's a girl to do?

A tattered old journal whispers secrets of yore,
While shadows all dance; I can't take anymore!
With every new giggle, I stumble with glee,
In the land of the quirky, I'm wild and I'm free.

So I navigate laughter, my guide to the fun,
In the attic of wonder, we're never all done.
With each silly mishap, my heart feels so light,
I'll explore every corner, through day and through night

## **Jigsaw Puzzle of Dreams**

Pieces are scattered, like socks in the air,
Trying to fit in, is it this one? Or where?
Colors mix wildly, a vivid display,
Laughing at puzzles life throws on the way.

I turn them around, a corner I find,
A cheeky little grin, what chaos unlined!
The picture is blurry, but isn't that great?
Finding new pieces, as I'm playing with fate.

A cat steals a puzzle, oh what a delight,
Jumping on edges, causing harmless fright.
With giggles and snorts, we climb higher in cheer,
Creating new worlds, with nothing to fear.

So I smile at the mess of this jigsaw gone rogue,
In laughter, I wander; I'll carry my vogue.
Life's a fun puzzle, with pieces that roam,
In the land of the silly, I've finally found home.

# The Unfolding of a Mysterious Tale

A cat in a hat sings a song,
While penguins dance all night long.
The clock strikes twelve, what a strange sight,
As jellybeans fall from the sky, oh what a delight!

The toaster is whispering secrets so bold,
To the fridge who just sits there, feeling so cold.
And the couch joins in with a creak and a groan,
As they plot to send me out on my own.

The goldfish is plotting a daring escape,
With a map made of lettuce and a cape.
The dog barks loudly, tries to take flight,
But he trips on the rug and lands with a fright.

In this circus of chaos, I sit with a grin,
As the world keeps spinning, I just let it spin.
For in every moment of utter confusion,
Lies the beauty of life's eccentric fusion.

# The Space Between Certainty and Doubt

There's a sock in the garden, a shoe in the tree,
And I'm standing here wondering, could that be me?
The sun shines bright but the sky's turning gray,
As a chicken in boots leads the parade today.

I ask for directions, they point to the stars,
While llamas in top hats discuss life on Mars.
The sandwiches chatter about what to eat,
While I tie my shoelaces with half of a beat.

A riddle from the mailbox, a puzzle on the door,
I ask what it means, but I'm lost even more.
The garden gnomes nod with a wink and a snicker,
And I swear that the goldfish just told me a flicker.

Between certainty's grip and doubt's gentle sway,
I'm spinning in circles, oh where should I play?
With laughter and whimsy in this playful roundabout,
I'll dance through the chaos, there's joy in the doubt.

## Lost in the Whirlwind

A rabbit in glasses is reading a book,
While I trip on my own shoelaces, what a kook!
There's a whirlwind of whispers and giggles nearby,
As the moon plays hopscotch with the stars in the sky

The carpet is rolling like waves on the sea,
With a parrot squawking, 'Where's the nearest tree?'
A bicycle's juggling some colorful balls,
While the cat takes a nap as the mailbox calls.

The wind blows a tune of a jolly good prance,
As the laundry hangs out for a silly dance.
I twirl with delight in this topsy-turvy mess,
While the puddles giggle, oh what a success!

And in this confusion, I burst into laughter,
For the joy of the ride is what I'm after.
Lost in the whirlwind, but what does it mean?
In a world so absurd, I'm the jester, the queen.

## The Fog of Uncertainty

Stumbling through fog that smells like old cheese,
I find a lost spoon and a couple of keys.
A dog wearing sneakers is chasing a cloud,
And I'm just wondering if that's allowed.

Mistakes hear my name and they chuckle with glee,
While the plants whisper secrets they won't share with me.
The sun hides its face behind fluffy gray hats,
As squirrels perform acrobatics with bats.

With each step I take, I'm slipping and sliding,
While a sandwich with legs starts quickly gliding.
The fog clears a bit, revealing a tree,
With a sign that says, 'Welcome to the land of the silly!'

I dance through the haze, wrapped up in a grin,
Embracing the nonsense, letting chaos win.
For in the fog's embrace, I find light in the jest,
And the unknown is where I feel truly blessed.

## Puzzles with Missing Pieces

Jigsaw sprawled across the floor,
Colors clash, what's it for?
Edges don't seem to connect,
Guess I'm lost, what'd you expect?

A cat sits smugly on my lap,
As I try to mind the gap.
Pieces vanish, one, two, three,
Do I even need a key?

Instructions vague, or not there at all,
Directions murmur, in whispers small.
Laughter echoes, frustration trails,
Not a clue, yet still, I wail.

Tomorrow's puzzle in today's mess,
With every twist, I just guess.
Even the cat rolls its eyes,
I ponder life, under strange skies.

## The Quest for Lost Certainty

With a compass that spins around,
I seek what can't be found.
Maps lead to the land of blur,
Where certainty is just a slur.

Climbing hills of doubt and fear,
Each step, laughter, not a tear.
Friends are lost, but spirits high,
We wave goodbye to reason's lie.

In a forest thick with haze,
Mysteries dance in puzzling ways.
Trees are talking, or so it seems,
Reality breaks at the seams.

Adventure stirs, come what may,
Let's embrace this wild disarray.
With giggles shared and hearts so light,
The quest continues, day and night.

## Threads of Perplexity

A game of knots, a tangled yarn,
Pulled on ends, oh what a charm!
Knitting tales with dizzy glee,
Where are patterns, can't you see?

Fabric frays with every twist,
Logic hides in a foggy mist.
Socks that vanish, sweaters askew,
What was I trying to sew, who knew?

Colors clash in wild display,
Frustration grows, but I still play.
Laughter threads my clumsy hands,
As I trip through these strange lands.

At the end, if I'm ever there,
I'll wear my chaos, it's only fair.
For life's a quilt that's full of cheer,
Stitched with joy, and maybe beer.

## In the Realm of What Ifs

What if ducks can speak in rhyme?
What if toast could stop all time?
Questions loop in silly ways,
Brightening up the dullest days.

Each 'what if' spins a tale,
Of unicorns and ships that sail.
The moon's a cheese, the sun a bread,
Imagined worlds swirl in my head.

Pondering roads that twist and turn,
With every thought, new bridges burn.
Life's a riddle, a playful trick,
With every glance, and every flick.

So in this realm, let's just play,
With 'what ifs' leading the way.
For certainty is just a snore,
Let's keep wondering, who needs more?

www.ingramcontent.com/pod-product-compliance
Lightning Source LLC
Chambersburg PA
CBHW051641160426
43209CB00004B/749